SINEWS OF FLEECE

Pastoral Poetry
with
Contextual Narrative

Clifford E. Bajema

TO SOW IS TO HARVEST

Scythe Publications, Inc.
A Division of Winston-Derek Publishers Group, Inc.

PUBLISHED BY SCYTHE PUBLICATIONS, INC.
Nashville, Tennessee 37205

Library of Congress Catalog Card No: 93-60418
ISBN: 1-55523-628-6

Printed in the United States of America

To Faith Ann,
who gentles me
and makes me strong.

To Sharon . . .
for your strong,
gentle spirit!
I love you!
Mildred Koning
mk♡

". . . as servants of God we commend ourselves in every way
. . . by purity, knowledge, forbearance, kindness, the Holy
Spirit, genuine love, truthful speech, and the power of God;
with the weapons of righteousness for the right hand and for
the left."

2 Corinthians 6:4,6-7

". . . we had courage in our God to declare to you the gospel
of God in the face of great opposition. . . . But we were gen-
tle among you, like a nurse taking care of her children."

1 Thessalonians 2:2b,7

"He has showed you, O man, what is good; and what does
the Lord require of you but to do justice, and to love kind-
ness, and to walk humbly with your God."

Micah 6:8

TABLE OF CONTENTS

INTRODUCTION

On the door of my office appear the words of the poem "Soft":

Soft as a vesper song,
compassion's voice
whispers welcome,
sedates my flurried feelings
taut with worry.

Soft as puppy fur,
compassion's touch
mellows my frame,
revives the petting felicity
to hands fisted by fury.

Gentle me, Love,
Supple my will;
hug me round
with sinews of fleece
and eiderdown.

Deeply felt human needs deserve more than trite reception and treatment. Responsive listening is not trite; easy answers are. Tender toughness is not trite; sentimental acquiescence or judgmental prescriptiveness are. "Severe mercy" (Sheldon Van Auken) is not trite; but soft empathy without tough principle is.

Hurting people need healing pastoral care and counseling of truthful encouragement. They need to be "gentled" but not indulged, hugged but not smothered with compromises. They need what Christ would give them if he could meet them directly at their places of pain and administer the healing touch of his soft, strong hands.

In fact Christ does so meet the broken. But he does this in and through his body which is the Christian Church. Of that body I am privileged to be a living member.

As a particular member of Christ's body I have been called to the pastoral office and have been endowed with a few special gifts which I am commissioned to use as a means of extending Christ's principled love. One of those gifts is poetry.

Obviously, writing a poem for someone is not always the preferred approach to a pastoral care situation. Nor is it ever enough in and by itself. But in some special cases it can become an ally to grace because it matches passion with passion, tears with tears, not just thoughts with thoughts. Faith is not pat answers captured best in logic or propositional statements. It is something living, and seems best expressed at times in the art of poetry, as the Psalms so eloquently testify.

Poetry is also a surprisingly commodious medium for striking a happy balance between softness and strength. It has such potential to add a nuanced sensitivity to one's pastoral care. Quite simply, it touches people: sometimes with the authority of a sword dividing and discerning the intentions of their hearts, and sometimes with the gentle stroke of a feather soothing their quivering spirits.

Maybe that's why so much of the Bible is poetry. Its words of judgment and redemption, of rebuke and comfort, are truly ministrations of painful healing through the merciful, two-edged scalpel of that great physician whom the poet T.S. Eliot called "The wounded surgeon."

My poetry falls far short of the infinite creativity and healing power of the inspired word of God. But at least it isn't art for its own sake, or art for the sake of a small cadre of elite literary professionals, hidden from the average person's view by its deliberate esoteric content or lack of any meaningful content. Poems should not be sterile art, mere rimes and rhythms and splashes of verbal color without meaning. The beauty of words, uniquely arranged, yet without *telos*, is shallow indeed. For me, poems may very validly arise out of and participate in the unfolding drama of redemption being played out on the heart stages of people questing for God's love.

Every poem in this volume has its story or context of sorts. It arose in response to someone's need (pain, grief, joy, etc.) or to an intense experience and was written to hug someone round "with sinews of fleece and eiderdown."

PART ONE: STUDENTS

Over the past twenty-five years my path of involvement with students has taken me to the University of Colorado, Kent State University and the University of Wisconsin in Madison.

Throughout most of those years I have maintained a connection with the academic community even though not always in direct, full-time campus ministry. My association with the InterVarsity Christian Fellowship organization through a three-year staff assignment and through teaching at many of their conferences, retreats, and leadership training camps has also been a constant vital link with students for me.

All the poems in Part One were written for college-age young people, although the themes have relevance to most any age. The names of individuals and incidental details which might bring risk of exposure have been changed.

Coming from a dysfunctional family and launching into the breathtaking freedom of a university community where the only moral restraints are those self-imposed, can leave a young, attractive coed extremely vulnerable. How can she, with all her social hunger and adolescent restlessness, resist the opportunity for intimacy with that young man who appears so tender and understanding and intelligent and available?

Melissa didn't. The scars that were left when the premature relationship inevitably ended in hurt and betrayal were brutal. Would another live-in malefriend be the answer to the deep loneliness and unrest inside? A second failure only brought more disillusionment.

Relationships, even with the anticipated bonding benefits of physical intimacy, cannot survive when they are sustained by vacuous hearts and minds devoid of a sense of spiritual identity and purpose.

Melissa needed to discover herself and find her true identity in God before she could even begin to think of a lasting relationship with a man. But for this discovery to occur, she needed to find a quiet place of refuge from the pressures and allurements of men. She needed to take a vow of chastity for a spell and retreat within herself to find out what and who she was vis-a-vis her God.

Such a place was not a retreat center somewhere in the north woods. Melissa's convent was the university where she had to learn to find God in the thick of things: in the middle of the intellectual challenge of the classroom, the blatant licentiousness of the dormitory, the empty emotional fervor of the stadium and the bustle of the commons. Her quiet place had to be the eye of the hurricane.

Slowly, by her living in prayer, meditation and watchfulness at a constant level of spiritual consciousness in the middle of a world falling apart philosophically and morally, she found a deep friendship with God. This settled the restlessness arising out of her profound loneliness. She found a true friend who would never exploit, manipulate, diminish or desert her.

Sometime in the middle of Melissa's hurt, when all was yet in disarray, and wounds were yet bleeding openly, and Melissa was just beginning to take her journey to that place of solitude where to find God and herself, I as her counselor felt a strange, mystical connectedness to her. Even when she left my office after another session, I could somehow follow her and be with her. Our spirits could "touch at distance."

I believe the poem "Solitude," given to Melissa when the night was yet dark, was an encouragement.

There is a quiet place
of mystic, pure communion,
of aloneness pulsating with presence
where our spirits can touch at distance.

There is a quiet place,
an eye in the hurricane, moving,
where, through uprootings and seizures of thought,
we can know, be known.

I feel from far away
the tremor of your private tears,
catch your missed heartbeat
in a fortissimo of gossip.

I pick up your whimper, sad,
in a room of raucous cheer,
sense the inflection of your heart breaking
when everyone's laughing, fickle.

Together in melancholic harmony of spirit,
embrasive aloneness,
let's fill the central emptiness,
reach across the void of loneliness.

In the hills of Tennessee, somewhere between Nashville and Chattanooga, runs a stretch of road with a prolonged downgrade hazardous to trucks with heavy loads. At certain marked intervals the State of Tennessee has constructed runaway ramps where the trucks which have gathered too much momentum can be driven off to the left and brought to a stop safely.

While traveling though those hills recently, I thought of a runaway, sensate culture out of control, picking up a head of steam on a steeply graded path of sexual license, and certain to flatten the lives of more than a few innocent souls who happen to be in the way. The escape ramps provided by religious faith, redirecting sex into wholesome, person-respecting channels, all seem to be ignored as though they are just distracting exits to cheap clothing outlets or fireworks supermarkets.

At the tender age of seven already, a little girl by the name of Sydney got in the way of her sex-driven father who, like a Mack truck with a full load of incestuous fantasies and with little moral restraint of conscience to brake himself, ran her over one dark, November night and many dark, cold nights thereafter.

Now, each year when the daylight hours shorten at the dawn of winter, Sydney lapses into a bleak depression. The terrifying, confusing memories of those years between seven and thirteen are more difficult to repress in November. Self-blame, false guilt and suicidal ideation all seem more persistent now for Sydney. The night-marish dreams become more frequent as well.

It was on one such gray day in November, when Sydney, now a college Senior, was sitting there in my office, all curled up into her withdrawn self, that the following words came to me for her:

As hours of dark
lengthening
bully the light moments away,
and trees stark naked shiver
over their leaf-skirt pile,
all the while you
strain to postpone
the inner sunset
of joy.

Comes every year
at this time:
the November depression,
a sense of ill
blackening the will
to be well,
a kind of psychic hell
stripping your soul
to nil.

I take your hands,
cold to the marrow,
and try to hug them warm
to my heart.
I try to fit a costume of pride
to your shame,
to light a candle
lasting 'til
darkness ends.

BALANCE BEAM

Some average people seem to find their places quite comfortably right in the middle of the pack. But others wear their averageness uneasily. The imagined idealistic expectations of God, friends or family (but in fact imposed by self on the self) can set up these average types for certain hurt and failure.

Leah was one such average student—average in beauty, intelligence and most other attributes—who often suffered under her okay status. At times she chafed at it, and at other times she would exaggerate all the negatives.

I wonder if this syndrome would have ever stopped if Leah had not, one day, found her true sense of self worth in the forgiving, affirming love of Christ.

It was during the summer of the Olympics that Leah stood up before the Church to make her public profession of faith. To memorialize her moment of significance, I found the image of the balance beam from the televised women's gymnastics competition to be an apt metaphor.

Can the stunningly beautiful
and cunningly bright
ever know the precarious plight
of balancing with but average gifts, at height,
trying to stand so boldly tall,
but teetering in emotional vertigo

8

between delusions of perfection
and illusions of rejection,
stumbling over fantasy ideals
or crumbling into the savage real?

But now a Love above
suspends you forgivingly in place,
helps you dance the narrow way
with such postured style and grace
that even you, surprised, amazed,
dismount to join the chorused praise
swelling from admiring witnesses,
echoing in descant the anthem welling
from celestial space: rejoicing all
for the beautiful who you are.

It's good to see you standing tall,
boldly upright and face unashamed,
readied for life's performance call,
steadied by the hand that lets you be
the best and only you.
There is none better.

CHANGING

Marriage is not the end-all and be-all of life, and single-ness can be distinctly fulfilling. But living single as a young man approaching thirty and still longing for an inti-mate life companion can also be intensely distressing.

This problem brought Alvin, a graduate student, to my office for counsel. Immediately I saw myself in Alvin. I remembered the rejections, the games, the self-doubt, the temptation to put on a front and pretend to be someone else, someone better and bigger than the real me.

Of course, it didn't work to pretend. A fabricated self is never as attractive as the original, natural self. So gradually I needed to change, not my self, but my tendency to hide or distort my self. I needed to change my habit of trying to change who I was and just learn to be. I needed to learn to celebrate the beautiful person God made me to be in all my uniqueness. Then someone else could love me too.

Time, pain and prayer gradually brought this maturity. Through several months of solitude and meditation on the unconditional love of God for me, I came to a wholesome self-acceptance. Then came the woman who was to be my wife. I could be myself and love myself when I was with her. She loved me too!

All this I passed on to Alvin, as I could see signs of the same change occurring in him.

10

Still missing, the
simple joys of lovers
kissing,
holding hands and eyes,
facegazing with obvious delight,
remain your desperate fantasy.

Women—in your eyes—
lovely enough
to compel affection
remain illusive,
become abusive
with ready excuses
of sudden busyness.

But time and pain
are dredging out the sludge
of awkward responses,
of immature behaviors,
transforming perceived shallowness
into a green depth.

Soon your pure waters
will lure a maiden wise to
draw deeply and drink.
She, refreshed,
could not then think

you were ever anything
but what you are.

Then will be love.

Holiday seasons are always such dreaded times by those whose fractured, dysfunctional families have left them feeling cut off and alienated.

Early in December already, Daniel felt the panic of Christmas coming on. Everyone should be with family at Christmas, shouldn't they! So Daniel, armed with an airline reservation, called his only sister, trying to arrange a visit. She explained she couldn't give Daniel much time because her boyfriend was going to spend the holidays with her. Maybe, she suggested, Daniel could come on December 31st. But not if he expected her to pick him up at the airport right in the middle of her New Year's Eve party. Forget it, thought Daniel. I feel like flying to Paris, but I can't afford it.

Visiting his mom out East wasn't an option either. She had recently written him a letter and called him a "lunatic" for mentioning that he believed in Jesus. Of course, Daniel's father was completely out of the question as a person to visit. He had left the family when Daniel was but a young boy, and had made it clear on numerous occasions since that he was too busy to have a relationship with his son. In fact Daniel felt his father was ashamed of him; for whatever reason, Daniel didn't know. Maybe he was too aesthetic, not sports-minded, or business-minded, or male-minded enough. Maybe he was just an inconvenience to his father.

Most of the time one can forget about slights and loneli-
nesses. But holidays always seem to bring deep wounds
directly to the surface. My spirit ached for Daniel. I
couldn't be his dad, or mom, or sister. But I could be his
friend and hold him in my heart. If only I could make him
trust me enough to believe that such friendship love was
possible. Maybe a poem would help.

That aerie "what's up?" manner of yours:
it doesn't hide the hurt
shown in wounded eyes, any more than
your burgundy hair belies blackness at the roots.

Some think you flit along effortlessly, gaily, brightly,
like a butterfly swept by gently swirling breezes,
but they can't see the gray cocoon
still wrapped around your orphaned heart.

Will the next shift of wind drive you
on impulse to Paris or Frisco or Jersey?
Each place is an imagined flower where you can rest
and wait for . . . mother, sister, friend, lover?

Always they are too busy chasing elusive selves
to ever think to link with you. You must
catch them on the fly in those places,
or touch wings in tenuous aerial dance.

14

But don't expect to clasp your weary wings
in soul embrace with them.
They're off again to find themselves
before you can be held.

Sit here awhile, then, my friend.
This is no Paris or Frisco or Jersey,
but I'm in no hurry,
and this love is no imagined flower.

By the time I met Alva, she had been through two hospitalizations and one suicide attempt in her battle with the eating disorder, anorexia nervosa and its later companion bulimia. She, a veteran of several years struggle already, knew far more about the condition than I or many of her professional therapists.

In one of her early letters to me she wrote: "the hateful, self-deprecative feelings come so automatic and unharnessed. I've been through counseling extensively and I know much about what and why I react in certain ways, but I haven't acquired the ability to stop the reactions before they happen. My intentions don't always meet the outcomes because of the fury I get caught in when trying to communicate with those who love me most. My hurting others causes me to feel guilt and it feeds the cycle of hurting myself in return."

In two other early communications she described her empty, hungry self:

"Emptiness"
Emptiness I feel
Looking deep within myself.
Eyes staring through the darkness of my soul.
Beads of sweat on my forehead,
Eyes bloodshot;

16

Self-induced purge.
Empty stomach—empty soul.
Surely Christ has left me,
I feel so empty now.
Weakened, I fall to my knees;
No joy,
No tears,
Just emptiness I feel.

"Hungry Self"
Do I eat for hunger?
Do I eat for taste?
Just look at the inches I'm adding to my waist.
Food for celebration.
Food for pain and strife.
Eating is the center of my calculated life.
Fighting back the pain.
Holding back the tears.
Flushing away the emptiness I've felt so many years.
I hate myself for failing.
I hate my body too.
Shattered self seeking peace—what am I to do?

I'm not sure what made Alva come to me. Perhaps it was an inner hope she spoke of and described as "driving me toward healthier thought and spiritual wellness." A.W. Tozer in *The Pursuit of God* had planted this hope in Alva's mind when he said: "God is so vastly wonderful, so utterly and completely delightful that he can without anything other than himself, meet and over-flow the deepest demands of our total nature, as mysterious and deep as it is."

Alva, in desperate pursuit of God as her last and only hope, was inexorably headed for what she described as her "Dark Night Blessing":

Dark night of the soul
Laid to rest by the Master's hand
Inner turmoil gives way
To spiritual freedom.

Dark night of the soul
In solitude I turned to him
Self-centered emotion stripped away
Brings inner transformation.

Dark night of the soul
Stilled by the power of his love
In the deep work of God
Comes peace, comfort, healing.

Dark night of the soul
Drawn away from all distraction
Appetites darkened, constrained
I see God's grace.

Dark night of the soul
Blessed experience.

In a subsequent letter to me she gave further evidence of healing: "Slowly I feel that Christ is reaching into my sheltered psyche and he is pulling out all the pain, guilt, anger, frustration and hopelessness. . . ."

The healing transformation of Alva, surely a miracle, was entirely God's work. My supportive role as friend and confidant over three years time was to point her to God, to be the conduit of his unconditional love. From me Alva simply looked for, in her words:

Gentle hand
Soothing touch
Smiles that reach my soul
Warm glow
Friendly face
Strength that makes me whole
Peaceful heart
Loving kindness
Support to reach a goal.

One of the simple supports I extended to Alva was the poem, "Anorexia," in which I sought to incorporate a delicate mixture of sinews and fleece:

Wily mirror
lies to your eyes,
shows gross rotundity
in sharp angles of bone,
tells you
God botched the creation—
yours in any case—
though an infinite beauty
of holy, wholly otherness
looks back at you hauntingly
and disputes the lie.

Throw away the glass!
Look at me!
I say, look at me
reflecting back to you
a truer image.
Borrow what I proudly show
to love yourself.

If I were the God
who made you,
I'd leap to my feet,
dance in the street
for joy of remembering
the very first thought of you.
Think it with me.

20

What joy a later grateful response from Alva brought me, confirming to me the miraculous healing power of divine love!

Dear Friend,

Thank you for believing in me when I found it hard to believe in myself.

Thank you for saying what I've needed to hear sometimes instead of always what I've wanted to hear.

Thank you for siding with me and for giving me another side to consider in life.

Thank you for keeping me from taking myself or my struggles too seriously.

Thank you for not laughing at me when I was too fragile to laugh at myself.

Thank you for being kind to me.

Your human compassion is enlivened
    By divine love
Through which my soul is able
    To rise above
A life of self-condemnation.
Your tears come from the soul;
    Touched by Christ,
You weep in joy that I am
    Brought to life
Through the light of the Cross.
Your prayer has life-giving power,

A true gift
That heals my inner wounds.
    No longer adrift
I'm linked to God's empowering graces.
Thank you, friend in Christ,
    Channel of salvation,
Through which I have seen love
    In his creation.
I'm grasping life anew.

Glory be to God! Even anorexia, as tenacious as its hold can be, resistant to all therapy, cannot sustain its defense when forced to a showdown with the love of Christ.

Our InterVarsity Christian Fellowship group had sponsored a public showing of the film *The Gospel According To Saint Matthew.* Produced by a group of Italian Communists, this film's portrayal of Christ's teaching and ministry was probably the most authentic I'd ever seen. The Communists seem to have understood toughness and commitment better than Hollywood script writers. The sinews of Christ were not covered with robes of sentimentality or pictured as the ever-hugging arms of Leo Buscaglia.

At any rate, a student named Shanna was found by Christ that night after viewing the film. To those of us who were present to hear her testimony, she spoke of a life in constant flight from God. Whatever there was to experience in the line of drugs, alcohol and sex she had tried. But to her amazement "the hound of heaven" kept after her in her downward plunge. Whenever she hit bottom, which was repeatedly, God would be there, waiting.

A few days after Shanna's conversion, I wrote for her the following hieroglyphic poem:

The
thrill
of
each
new

fumbling
for
a
possible
happiness
in
the
jumbling
of
life's
alternatives
seems
always
to
be
tumbling
me
downward
over
jagged
rocks
where
in
the
spill
is
always
Him

24

DEAR AGNOSTIC FRIEND

Tom, an agnostic graduate student of philosophy who I eventually came to know as a friend, reminded me of a mountain goat. He had become a swift, elusive prey, while I was a clumsy, noisy hunter trying to get near him with the tactics of rational arguments and sensible apologetics. But Tom was always clever and intellectually nimble enough to keep me out of range.

Eventually I realized that only love would bring us close.

Dear agnostic friend:

Your words, so smooth,
like hoofed airfoils,
invite recoil
upon their surface.

Your face, so smiling,
yet white with fear,
accents crevice
of black despair.

Your thoughts, so light,
like balloons blown tight,
do pop away in thinner air
before I understand.

Drop your guard,
my sparring friend,
and give me the height
to set you free in sight
                    of love,
                    Cliff.

Three Poems To Samara

From the first day that Samara stepped into my campus ministry office with her questions and challenges, I knew she was experiencing an intense spiritual struggle. Disheartened and disillusioned from all the dead-end adventures of an explorative life style, Samara began to sense within her soul a deep hunger for Christ, who at once allured her and alarmed her.

In the course of many conversations Samara chose to allow me to see to the deep reaches of her faith struggle. To be asked to enter the combat arena of another person's life and death encounter with God is awesome, for it is an invitation to holy ground. The ground is made holy by the spillage of much blood and tears from the open wounds of living.

The three poems to Samara which follow grew out of our discourse. They were responses to Samara's ambivalent pursuits and wary flights ("Pursuit"), her convictedness of moral corruption ("The Good Soil"), and her fears that the old demons would continue to hurt and control her ("This Darkness Past").

"Pursuit"
If you're the fox pursued,
then am I the rabbit sacrifice
distracting you to the Hound?

Gladly would I die
if I could make you lie, waiting
the Hound's uplifted stroke of love.

So run after me with slyness.
What else can a fox do?
I'll run you to Our Highness.

Maybe . . .
How much chase is in you?
Do I dare leave my warren?

"The Good Soil"

You're no vacuous, creatureless shell
emptied of squirming spiritual life,
no water-flushed porcelain bowl
dreading the next foul dropping.

You're the good soil, nature's decay,
blackened, yea, into a rich compost
of rotted fruit and leafage spoil,
fermenting an organic passion.

Out of fallenness mingled together
into one composite of body, mind and spirit

28

rises fresh green stems artfully exploding
into white untouched blossoms.

Within the floral temples I spy
those fragile pink stamens lying
and know that these are you, finest and fairest,
waiting to birth beauty from the dying.

"This Darkness Past"

Devilish shadows
slither
stealthily behind,
silent,
evasive,
crouching cowardly
behind mossy roots
of brooding cedars,
crawling belly-down
in swampy grasses,
poised for paralyzing strike
at vulnerable moment
when back is turned
and feet are slowed
by terror.

Fiendish faces of fear
haunt the night.

Whispers a hissy hollow voice:
Your newness can't last.
You are what you are
what you are
what you are
and what you have been
is what you will be
will be
will be.
Your prison is your past
for you belong to me.

Clammed up in a dark forest,
damned to run impulsively
into thickets of despair?
Damned to slide
down
sensuous
paths
to slam the rocks below?

Stop, worship!
Remember and believe
that venom-laced hell of the Dying One

30

has crushed that head
whose faces are but vapors
signifying nothing,
whose voice is reverberation
of your own self-accusation.

In the name of Christ
comes peace
in dark places,
comes future
to your past.

Guests had come over to share a Saturday night dinner with us. Just after we were seated, I took sick. The aroma of the spaghetti and garlic bread (a favorite meal) only antagonized my nausea. Finally I had to dismiss myself.

Although I, like St. Paul, prefer to believe my citizenship is in heaven, such celestial thinking has not quite relieved me of various vestigial interruptions to my state of well-being, such as coming down with the flu, which was the case that Saturday night.

Sickness has a way of robbing me of all my stoical toughness and reducing me to a helpless baby. I understand this is almost a universal phenomenon with men! At any rate, my good wife took me by the hand, led me to the couch, untied my shoes, brought me a pillow, covered me with a blanket and put a thermometer in my mouth.

From that time, on, and all through the night, I experienced discomfort and could not sleep. The strange thought occurred to me at some odd hour of the night: maybe there was something I could learn about ministry to people from this unpleasant experience!

And these were my thoughts: Although I am ill and the mere thought of food causes my stomach to do cart-wheels, I know that sooner or later I must eat again. My mortal flesh will obligingly prove its mortality if I withhold daily bread. So what do I do? Get out of bed and ransack the refrigerator? Obviously not. The mere thought makes my nausea promptly return. Right now, at this particular moment, I do not need food. The ultimate (daily bread) will have to wait until such time as it can once again be tolerated. So what do I need? Precisely what I am getting— rest, a blanket, a thermometer, a pillow, a kiss on the cheek from my wife. I need penultimate mercy. Morning will come soon enough, and then perhaps, I can begin to sip a little broth.

And what does all this teach me about ministry to people? It makes me think that maybe some of the people who come to hear me preach on Sundays are probably too sick to feed from the ultimate meal of grace. It nauseates them, and they avoid the Church. Could it be that what they need, at the present moment, is the loving concern of a neighbor, a deacon or a friend to help them overcome their spiritual flu symptoms? Could it be they need an outstretched hand and a pat on the shoulder? Can the ultimate message of salvation possibly have any effect on them if it is not preceded by penultimate acts of mercy and concern? Can I really help people if I preach justice but do not love kindness?

The next morning, as the spoonfuls of soup slipped slowly into my mouth, I wrote the following poem entitled "Penultimate Mercy":

33

Souls' sickened, shivering bones
and fevered, freezing feet
stumble up cathedral stones
to dine with health's elite.

The offer there is lamb of life,
the prime-grade cut of grace;
but like a grating garlic knife
it grieves the stomach's face.

Nausea is the soul's sick froth,
no cure for which is meat,
for its aroma from the cloth
draws vomit to the feet.

If souls have feet and feet have souls
and souls are sick when feet are froze,
then first for feet should care the Cloth
and souls can start to sip their broth.

The miracle of modern medications for pain has put tremendous power into the prescription-writing hands of physicians and increasing pressure on their good judgment. For obviously, their pharmaceutical cures can do wonders, but can also lead to the new sickness of dependency.

The worst of all possible worlds is when drugs are no longer strong enough to allay pain and yet so potent as already to have produced an addiction. Then when withdrawal from drugs, with no certain hope of the original pain-producing problem having been solved, becomes the only recourse, the journey ahead becomes excruciatingly difficult, to say the least.

Kerry would come to my office in obvious pain, clutching her head, having had no momentary relief from relentless headaches for days, even weeks. She came needing something to help her cope. Her medications had to be cut down, for her own health's sake and to protect her unborn child. Yes, on top of everything else, Kerry was pregnant.

When pain is really intense and has been ravaging its victim for a long time, the sense of where it is coming from becomes vague. Talking about it seems difficult. Somehow pain succeeds in stifling the very words which can name and tame it. This is true not only for the pain-carrier but also for the friend or counselor who tries to be a pain-receiver. Nothing can be said. There is little to do but just to feel, to company with, to pray—sometimes silently. Perhaps the following poem helped Kerry know that at least some small measure of her pain had been received and shared.

Something
down
deep
is
torn
somewhere.

Through
open
fizzure
blood
flows
frenzied.

Persistent
pounding
hammers
your
head
numb.

Its
sound
no-one
hears
but
you.

Mere
whisper
from
me
startles
fear.

Even
my
loving
hands
look
lethal.

And
you
recoil
holding
your
face.

37

Space
I
give
you
then
quietly.

No
help
from
touch
or
speech.

Only
just
being
there
will
do.

PART TWO: ADOLESCENT TEENS

Adolescents, at every stage, have always compelled my interest, though they are not the easiest age group with whom to establish trust. Junior high and high school kids especially require from us adults an approach of honest frankness if we are to have any hope of penetrating their facade of indifference and boredom. They respond positively to a balanced message of tough love. If the love isn't tough, adolescent teens can be master manipulators. If the toughness isn't loving and the sinews of correction and direction have no feel of fleece, teens can be insensitive and mean-spirited.

They are also remarkably appreciative of creative communication, like the use of poetry in a story context. The poetic selections which follow are among those which God has especially and repeatedly blessed as I've presented them orally at numerous gatherings of teens.

Again, wherever names appear, they are pseudonyms.

THE FREAKS, THE JAYCEES, AND ME

In the years of the late 60's and early 70's, I spent most of my time ministering on the streets to adolescent youths in the drug culture who came by the thousands to Boulder, Colorado where I was living at the time. I watched the freaks and summer hippies pass their junk and hasten over to every free food line. I listened as they idly strummed their guitars while talking of Hare Krishna and horoscopes and demonic powers. I sat by as their minds (drugged with speed, STP, LSD or heroin) slowly turned to swiss cheese and their hearts to melancholy.

Sometimes I could help, but most of the time the irrational-escapist atmosphere seemed to close all channels of constructive communication. At those times, I knew afresh how hard it is to go on loving, even such as these wandering waifs of the counter culture.

After one particularly frustrating day on the streets, I returned home to the therapy of writing down my thoughts in poetry:

I sat with the freaks
    on dirty asphalt curbs
    and store-front steps
and caught short glimpses
    of hands so quickly
    passing on

encapsuled hopes of high escapes

from sexual boredom

and meaningless talk

of things so cool

and such and such.

I traced with Tom astrology charts

and whiffed with Mary sweet incense fumes

while listening too

to voodoo songs

and following nomad eyes

on wandering courses.

And I thought, God,

What is there now that I can do?

After that draining summer of ministry to the counter culture ended, I went on a much-needed vacation and traveled east with my family. We chanced to stay at a Holiday Inn in Council Bluffs, Iowa where the Jaycees were having their national convention. All through the night these respectable representatives of the dominant culture treated us to an exhausting display of carousing: boozing and giggling and joking suggestively in the hallway outside our door. The next morning the elevators were broken and the trash containers overflowing with beer cans and the hallways strewn with bales of hay, brought in to add a comfy, barn-like atmosphere to the convention.

I left the motel that next morning weary and fighting my hostile feelings, this time towards the hypocrites of the dominant culture. My feelings came to poetic expression in these words:

I heard the Jaycees
    (belching through my motel door
    at 3:00 A.M.)
laughing on their bales of hay-
    hauled into the Holly Inn
    to add a touch of haymow play
    to an already suggestive spin
    of pinching here and goosing there-
and cursing damnable hippies
    who dirty up the towns
    of respectable men
    (belching through my motel door
    at 3:00 A.M.)
And I thought, God,
    What is there now that I can do?

Well, I observed the freaks and it seemed I saw the Jaycees. I observed the Jaycees and it seemed I saw the freaks. I observed them both and it seemed I saw myself. I observed myself and it seemed I saw mankind. And I was perplexed. And I thought, God, what is there now that I can do?

And then it came to me. Before I try to do anything, I should first of all request God's forgiveness: for myself, and for those whom I resemble. And then I should go on loving, even such as these unloveable, with as much patience as I would readily grant myself. For God's love extends to the freaks, the Jaycees and yes—even to me! And if God loves me, then to be sure, his love is worldwide, indiscriminate, for I am the chief of sinners.

God is far more hurt than I am over the indifference of people to himself. But he doesn't give up. Neither does he batter people into submission. He is longsuffering. His love is limitless. And so should be mine, by his Spirit.

TWO POEMS FOR THE DRUG CULTURE

When school officials in a small rural town in Wisconsin discovered an alarming number of drug syringes in their high school's waste baskets, they became aware of what many in the larger cites like Detroit, New York and Milwaukee already knew—that the drug problem among youth is nearly out of control.

It was in the mid sixties, as the last third of the twentieth century began, that drugs seemed to become a special attraction to youth. Drug usage in the sixties and early seventies, though it ultimately sabotaged the ideals of the counter-cultural hippies, was nevertheless linked to a search for a higher consciousness, a deeper and more compelling spirituality. Drug usage was part of a comprehensive protest against the isolating materialism of the dominant culture, as expressed in the following poem:

"Sixties Hippies"

Split from fathers
buying love with credit cards
for empty sons and daughters
gased nigh to death with things
they never wanted.

44

Split from scenes
of plastered bone-white walls
and knick-knacks bunched on shelves
and tailored suits and gowns
and plastic cells in prison towns.

Split from harsh,
competitive spirits
of parental hearts
calloused thick beyond compassion
by the upward crawl to material merits.

Fled on fragile hopes
to lonely streets
where tired legs and outstretched thumbs
acquired sufficient passport
to freedoms hoped for.

Fled to homely places where,
in blank despair, they crashed
in festering heaps of family flesh
all bandaged in by adhesives thin
of communal love and peace.
Fled, it's said,
to nature's theater,
super market,

school and temple
all in one.

Found a proclivity
for sterile productivity
in spiritual monasteries
of unreality—
getting it together.

Found, it would seem,
a more primitive scheme
of material value,
exhausting their steam—
begging for survival.

Found, one would say,
that chemical way
of leeching love's ration
so desperately needed
for re-creation.
Wretch or weep—the question.
And for whom,
a suggestion?
For myself, maybe,
for failure.

But now in the nineties drug usage is wedded to a deep pessimism. Drugs are an escape from the real; they are no longer a window to some sought-after ideal. In a culture where public institutions of learning have been stripped of theism and of any notion of absolute moral values, where nothing makes sense and where hope for a better tomorrow—either in this world or in the next—has utterly died, drugs make it unnecessary to think and make anything add up. Drugs are an entree to immediate sensual gratification in the present. And the present is all that really counts. Drugs are a magical, chemical way to simulate a perpetual orgasmic experience. In a society literally wallowing in an orgy of sexual consciousness, drugs have tremendous appeal for a stimulated group of adolescents in need of another momentary ride into euphoria.

Will the last third of the twentieth century be one day described in history books (assuming some kind of histories will still be written) as the tri-decade when a whole generation of youth were wiped out by drugs and sex-related diseases?

The failure of this era is the failure of all of us to see where our brave new world of sexual consciousness and freedom is taking us and our youth. It is as though a whole generation of youth is "sitting on a public bench in clear display of certain sinking," and all we seem to be able to give them is more talk of liberation, more free condoms, more disparagement of delayed gratification, and less opportunity to learn about God and his health-producing, life-preserving moral order for the universe.

"Drug Addict"

Today I saw a spirit dying,
sitting on a public bench
in clear display of certain sinking.

The lad, he sat there,
slowly pumping his corpse-like body
in the rocking waves of some inner music;
and my call of love from far away
was met by empty stare
in mocking eyes (I now feel choked to say)
were clouded by an inner storm.

And I knew then, as now I feel,
how much adrift his life had been
since first he left his Father's shore.

But God, my tears, O God my tears,
will they seal up his mortal wound?

TO AN ALCOHOLIC DAUGHTER

The drug of choice for a young person today may not necessarily be crack cocaine. It may be, and often is, alcohol.

For Kristin alcohol became an addiction, and she ended up spending part of her junior year of high school in a detoxification/rehabilitation center.

Her parents vacillated in their feelings among anger, disappointment, guilt and pity. Finally at the end of Kristin's hospitalization, they came to me and expressed frustration about how to receive and what to say to their daughter. I sensed they truly loved Kristin, but just didn't know quite how to respond.

The poem which follows was my attempt to assist their response. I suggested they give it to Kristin as a homecoming note, which happily they did.

Like a precocious, pregnant bud
bursting into premature bloom in Spring,
you grew up too early our child.

    But, lo, the night is chilling
    and we fear the killing frost.

The beauty of the yellow daffodil seems
so short-lived, yet pleases us so
as the first-fruit of Spring's splendor.

You please us too, teenage woman-child,
please us with the blossomed-beauty of your smile,
your delicate mind and your special style.

The petals of music, poetry, art and love in you
have just begun to show their face,
just begun to turn their deeper hue.

But, lo, the night is chilling
and we fear the killing frost.

Come home, dear child, out of the night,
out of the guilt, out of the temptations
to which your tender spirit ought not be exposed.

Come home dear child, out of the cold,
and thrive in our warmer midst until
the summer's come and you be older still.

The association of youth and spring is a strong and natural one in my mind. Whenever the daffodils and robins reappear, I—almost instinctively and with a bit of melancholy—think back to my high school days when life was so full of virility and possibility.

If there is a day of salvation, a special time of ripeness for the fruit of spiritual commitment, it has to be the time of middle adolescence. In this time of life, the worms of cynicism have not yet hatched their larvae and the still-childlike openness to God has not yet calcified into skepticism and doubt.

So almost inevitably every spring I seize some available opportunity, whether in church or chapel, to address to adolescent teens the call of Qoheleth (the preacher in Ecclesiastes) to commitment. For as well I know, already myself at mid life, the spring quickly passes, followed all too hastily by the seasons of summer and autumn, and so soon there is winter.

Earth like the eagle
recovers her youth
under the May sun
with healing in his wings.

51

Winter shuffles out finally
to the utter relief of kids
weary of the old man's
whites and blacks and grays,
depressed by his dandruff
on their shoulders and
feeling smothered by all his blankets.

Kids love to play
outside
in T-shirts.

Welcome sun!
Welcome green and blue and yellow,
polished silver hub-caps,
sweaty brown shoulders,
orange beach towels
and youth again!

Now is the spring
and you are sixteen,
fresh as the birthing crocus
blooming purple,
alive as alive can be.

Energy multiplies like loaves and fish.
Strength lengthens like the days.

Awkwardness turns to agility.
Features soften,
blemishes slip away,
beauty surfaces through flesh and bone.
Your skin has the smell of apple blossoms;
your grip is firm;
your limbs feel alive, vigorous.
Your step bubbles spontaneously into a skip,
then explodes like a grasshopper.

A bearish stockmarket,
a wolfish grocery budget,
a lionish school tuition cost,
a giraffian orthodontist bill
are only animal pets to you,
tugging playfully at your feet
while driving your parents to distraction.

Desire stirs,
members respond,
hopes awaken.
A future of romance,
    work,
    procreation,
    invention,
    travel
awaits.

Cedar smells like cedar,
strawberries like strawberries.
You are sixteen,
alive and well.

Well?
Well . . . are you?

Soon will come the longer days of labor,
        heat,
        sweat.
Nights too hot to sleep sometimes.
Then a long summer mid-life of duty,
        responsibility,
        commitment.

You'll look for autumn:
time to smell the leaves,
listen to the wind
into the night
and watch the waves
lapping the shore of your retirement cottage
where you hope your health will let
you stay till winter and . . .

No one wants to be a shut-in.

No one wants to be put up with.

No one wants to be a needless expense.

The heart calcifies with age,

like the bones,

and can close itself to light,

      to truth,

      to new smells,

      new thoughts,

      new ideas,

      to God.

Remember now your Creator

in the days of your youth

before the evil days come

and the years draw nigh

when you will say:

I have no desire,

no space in my heart for him

who was so easy to love and believe

when it was Spring.

But I had not the sense to say,

I will.

Now it is winter.

It came to me one summer vacation day when I returned to my home in the State of Washington after many years of absence. I noticed there was an older look to my hands. The people in my little home town hardly recognized me anymore. The roof on my mother's house, which I had put on so few years ago it seemed, was now covered with moss, betraying the passage of time.

I'm getting older! I thought. And the realization prodded some questions in my mind: What is my life all about? Why do I eat, drink, sleep, play, vacation, learn, work? The spinning wheel of life continues to turn and I seldom jump off to ask the question why. What does all this mean? Is there some unified purpose in life which cuts across all the diversity of things people do during their brief earthly span of sixty to eighty years? Why am I alive?

The thought process, as described above, worked on my mind for several weeks. It even followed me eastward as I traveled to the campus of Princeton University to speak at a youth convention later in the summer. Finally the persistent pressure of the unanswered question forced me to sit down and write, out of which came a poem, "Spinning Wheel":

It's so easy to merry go round

merry go round

merry go round in an endless whirl

of busy things

never stopping the spinning wheel

for moments of reflection

    on the meaning

the meaning

        of having babies

        and discussing the Democrats

        and waiting for traffic lights

        on the way to meetings

        and working

        and showering

        and reading the New York *Times*

        and always eating

        and getting fat

        and growing old

        and dying of heart attacks

        in the middle of sex

            or Sanka

            or something

Yes it's so easy

not to think

and just to run and run and run
'til everything's done
and done
and undone

It's so easy to miss the sound
of the still small voice
that screams from out the tear-watered ground
of another's pain or loneliness

It's so easy to live
and live
and live
and live
and die
and never love

Live along
move along
bring up the line
Keep going
keep achieving
keep consuming
keep building
keep destroying

Analyze
propositionalize
creedalize
catechize
synthesize
rationalize
and finally just criticize

But do not love
do not love
For God's sake
do not love
for tomorrow you die

Here we go round the spinning wheel
the spinning wheel
the spinning wheel

And the still small voice
whimpers out of the dust and noise of the carnival
and knows there is only one Man
who will ever hear
the question of human pain
and answer with his life

"Spinning Wheel" was the beginning of my answer. But even more so was I relieved by the prayer that followed:

Jesus the Christ of God,
you are the one who heard the question
and answered with your life.
I sit motionless this moment
to give you thanks.

Liberate me from the spinning wheel
and set me free
to love with your caring heart,
and to hear with your sensitive ears
the still, small voices of need whimpering
out of the crazy busyness of life's carnival.

To that end, fill me now
with your blessed Spirit.

Just about the time I concluded my prayer, I noticed a high school girl, sitting in a darkly lit alcove of a college dormitory building, quietly weeping because she was rather fat and rather alone. She obviously wasn't the kind of person whom her friends stopped by to pick up on their way to the spiritual rock session at the convention hall.

As I sat down next to her to chat, I thought of Jesus of Nazareth who always listened for the still small voices of pain and need above the racket of life's carnival and sought out broken and lonely people to heal and love. I thought of this humble carpenter of Galilee, and I saw clearly once again the reason for living—to be a channel of his Spirit in bringing kindness, comfort, healing and truth to others. And I forgot about my hands, looking older every day.

Two Poems For The School Assembly

It happened most often on the school bus, as I remember. Mary Lou was teased from early childhood on through high school.

"Just Teasing"

She never made the honor roll,
She had white, stringy hair,
    thick glasses,
    poor posture,
    fallen arches,
    lousy coordination,
and was a perfect target for teasing
every time.

Her only problem
was that she couldn't answer back;
there was no wit or venom in her tongue.

And so, over the years,
she cried more and more,
privately,
and coughed incessantly from sheer nervousness,
and always wondered why her girl friends called

so seldom
and boy friends never.

She couldn't cope, Lord,
and now she is broken
and almost alone.

Will you pick up the pieces
and be a very special friend to her?

And will you forgive all those children
who enjoyed so many good laughs at her expense?

They didn't really know
what they were doing.
They didn't hear her crying every day
when she stepped off the school bus.

The emotional scars for Mary Lou today, as she in her fifties lives single, are still obvious, though ironically she devotes her life to the care of children. Now they don't tease her. She is like a mother to them, which is a good thing to have in this day and age when dads and moms are both out working.

Another girl in my school, Wilma, was so cruelly abused by teasing that just three weeks after entering high school she dropped out. When about a week of Wilma's absence had gone by, her mother showed up at the principal's office with the report that Wilma had stopped eating and was determined to starve herself. Wilma's mom wondered if something bad might have happened in the school. The principal asked around. We senior class boys knew right away why Wilma wasn't eating. She had been mercilessly teased and had lost her will to live. We promised the principal that if Wilma came back to school and started eating again, we would personally see to it that she would not be teased again. We even asked the principal for permission to deal directly with anyone who as much as looked cross-eyed at Wilma. He wisely gave us this authority. We never had to apply our lay discipline. The other kids were scared to death of us. With advocacy, Wilma survived.

Steve almost didn't make it. He was kind of an egghead, smarter than anyone in the school, but scrawny in appearance and quite inept socially. He was, as they say, a perfect target for teasing every time. The worst of many awful times was at a high school assembly one day. The guest speaker, for purposes of illustration, asked if the strongest, most muscular and macho male would come to the platform. Unbelievably, the student body began to chant, "Steve, Steve, we want Steve." Deeply embarrassed, but feeling immense peer pressure, Steve reluctantly went forward. The crowd cheered wildly. The speaker seemed blind to the ugly dynamics of what was going on.

64

Now Steve is a graduate student and his hatred for the students and teachers of that school still eats at his mind so much that his hostility is like a gangrene. It threatens to destroy him and has put a heavy mortgage on his future ability to relate normally to people. Fortunately Steve is dealing with his problem in counseling and is making real progress in releasing the bitterness. Yes, he has even written a letter to the school, these many years later, describing his hurt, but also offering his forgiveness.

A Christian junior high principal asked me a while ago to speak for his school's chapel. He requested that I talk about what I wished someone had said to me in a school assembly or chapel when I was that age. Well, I thought about Mary Lou, and then I thought about Wilma and Steve.

I decided that I wished someone had had the guts to come and speak to my school about murder by teasing. Could Jesus possibly have had school children in mind when he warned, ". . . whoever insults (says Raca to) his brother (or sister) shall be liable to the council, and whoever says 'You fool!' shall be liable to the hell (Gehenna) of fire"? Mary Lou, Wilma and Steve certainly had their share of "racas" thrown at them. But if Jesus meant what he said, this is serious business. So now I try to speak about this in schools, and sometimes I read to students the following poem:

"Praise The Other"

Seems more natural, friend,
to criticize.
Things done wrong
clamor for attention more greedily than
things done right.

I see you, friend,
in all your splendor and weakness!
And I wonder,
what makes me want
to trivialize the glory of you
and herald your defeats?
What makes me want
to bury your treasures
and publicize your debts?

Today I want to praise you, friend.
Simply and without restraint or envy,
I applaud your being there
and thank God for what you are—
as you are.

When I really look at you,
it's as though I'm viewing

a carbon copy of myself.
Everything I feel, you feel.
Your hands—they could be mine!
Everything about you is human,
and I participate in that same genus of being.

With what ease and dispatch
I can forgive myself the negatives
which render my humanness imperfect!
Can't I, with a view
to your flesh and blood sameness,
accord to you the same respect?

Today I want to praise you, friend.
Simply and without restraint or envy,
I applaud your being there
and thank God for what you are—
as you are.

PART THREE: PEOPLE OF THE PARISH

The church parish is not a magic kingdom. Church people hurt, they laugh, they play, they struggle, they need a physician, they get well, they die.

Whoever has a heart for the pastoral care of people will find that the entry points into the deeper levels of peoples' lives are multiple. The moment of transition from superficial acquaintance to knowing connectedness might be a sudden hospitalization, a psychotic episode, a shared experience of maddening injustice, of the ambiguity and agony of divorce or of frivolous fun with kids.

The church is a cross section of real people whose lives reflect at some point all that is part of real life. How often it has seemed to me that poetry has provided the eye to photograph what should be remembered or honored. How often poetry has provided just the right touch needed as a response in such real life situations: a touch soft yet steadying, or penitent yet rebuking, or light yet serious. Sinews of fleece come to mind again.

DUMB SHEEP

Philip Keller's *A Shepherd Looks At The Twenty-third Psalm* has been of immense help to me as I, on countless occasions, have been called to the hospital bedside of someone who has just experienced a heart attack, an injury, or a setback of some kind that has put her flat on her back for a while. The initial response of the stricken patient can be a kind of "why me" anger along with a restlessness to get back on her feet as soon as possible. The analogy of sheep being made to lie down by the shepherd is the insight from Keller I've found most relevant in such situations.

According to Keller, sheep need to chew their cuds to digest consumed grass. But sheep will not do this unless they are lying down. If the shepherd doesn't prevent them, the sheep will run to drink rather than lie down to chew. This causes bloat and death. I believe it was T.S. Eliot in *The Four Quartets* who spoke of "the absolute paternal care which will not leave us but prevents us everywhere."

I went out early
to graze in the green pastures of your goodness.
I ate my fill of blessing
and was just about gorged at mid-day.

70

Heavy of forage, I began to perspire,
trying to follow you in the heat of the day.
With an insatiable thirst for further blessing,
I felt insanely driven to the still waters
where I might have bloated myself
if you hadn't resisted me.

Thank you, good Shepherd,
for postponing my enjoyment of the still waters,
for making me lie down first,
thus enforcing the saliva rule.
Thank you for insisting that I chew my cud awhile
so as to digest your many blessings.

Thank you, wise Shepherd,
for all the times you've laid me down.
Sometimes it hurts a lot and I complain
because I want an immediate fill of the still waters.
But deep inside I know well enough
that grazing through life's pastures
without your severe mercy
is suicide.

BREAKDOWN

For a person who is anxious or depressed enough, a nervous breakdown must be a huge relief, even though it is a temporary and negative coping mechanism. For example, when the rockslide of mid-life crisis gangs up on a man and gets him all caught up in his own compulsive needs and irrational anxieties, it can pick up a momentum which makes him feel like pieces of himself are splintering off at every downward roll of his life. The frantic attempts to grab hold and retain a unity of self can be so exhausting that in time these efforts seem futile. Then the temptation to just let the mind freeze, to just give up, to stop trying to make sense of it all, becomes irresistible. The psychotic episode has begun. When this happened to Jim, I was there. I had been one of the people to whom he was desperately looking for an answer. When it didn't come fast enough or in a manner that Jim could receive, he found his own answer; he entered his own "analgesic shelter" (Dobson).

Of course, hospitalization for psychiatric care was the result. When, after a few weeks of therapy, Jim had much improved and was nearing the end of his confinement period, I left with him the following poem:

We watched you fall downhill:
your anxiety triggering your depression,
your depression tripping on your anxiety.
Over the smallest pebbles you stumbled
as ever lower you tumbled into yourself:
your mind agitated, unresponsive
to the body's demand for rest.

Every stone became a mountain
and every stubble of grass a forest
overwhelming you, enveloping you,
drawing you deeper into trouble,
darkness now the only familiar face.

Or was the phantom of darkness you saw
only the menacing face of
your employer sure to fire you,
your creditor sure to foreclose on you,
your wife sure to despair of you,
your children sure to judge you a failure,
your friend sure to avoid you?

Feeling your life was finished
and the purpose for living diminished,
you longed for death,
yet feared it more than ever.

For where was God?
And why didn't he respond?
Or was he maybe punishing you
by causing this despond?

Then your mental circuitry jammed,
and, though you still could hear voices
giving advice and expressing care,
you became too exhausted even
to escape the irrational snare.
Strength to whimper was hardly there.

At the bottom finally,
completely rolled into yourself,
looking like a battered child
crouched fearful in a fetal pose,
you stared blankly as we picked you up
and took you gently to a sheltered place
out of the pressures of the higher space.

Now we can only wait for God's response.
He is with you in the valley, we know,
and understands forsakenness full well.

Surely he will heal you in time
and make your spirit strong again.

And when your mind is as willing
as your body to brave the higher clime,
you will come out,
and with eyes set on him in trust,
begin anew the climb of life.

FOUR SEASONS

The last time I saw Lois Veenstra (actual name), she was a mere skeleton sitting in the passenger seat of her car, propped up with pillows so she could look out across the sunlit water, as her husband drove over the river channel leading to Lake Michigan. A look of radiance was on her thin, ghostly face. She obviously was delighted with the gift of one more day, of which she had few left, for she had terminal cancer.

Though Lois battled with cancer for several years, she did not allow her personal ordeal to rob her of an attitude of praise and a heart to serve others. Unfortunately, I was not able to complete the poem "Four Seasons" in time to give it to Lois before she died. Her husband accepted it posthumously on her behalf.

While others at the dawn
slept in and
cursed the imagined darkness,
you, hounded by immanent death,
went out to exalt one last sunbeam.

Such has always been your way:
to damn the demon winter
and rise to look for spring forever.

76

Some lesson
for we satiated summer folk
in our shaded recliners
who beckon with our bleak dissatisfaction
the early return of autumn clouds.

AFTERLIFE

I have stood next to many in their dying. Not once can I recall anyone, young or old, accepting lightly the ravaging of the body, or facing glibly and without due reverence the awesome moment of passing away. Though I have not yet stared death in the face, I have tried in the poem "Afterlife" to find a way to feel with the dying in their dread, fear, revulsion and impatience, while still pointing them through the darkness to the Person of Light.

At the last trumpet,
    will
    the
    tunnel
    of
    death
be a blackening black, then
        a cul-
        de-
        sac,
        a u-
        turn
        back
to the gray, perpetually
dying way
        of living?

Or will my swaddled wings find spread
    as soon as my cocoon is shed
      before the Light?

Flesh and blood cannot inherit
    the kingdom of heaven.

It is downright
    dishonorable
to be biodegradable,
      worthless as the dust
      gathering on a silver platter
      like the head of John the Baptist,
    two-dimensional,
    weak,
    living on borrowed energy,
    nothing more than a scaled-down model
      of something ultimate and
      multi-dimensional,
      life-generating,
      lifted out of the dishonor
          of
          a
          prior
          Fall.

Will I ever be the finished product,
   the newer, better, second-Adam self,
   powerful, spiritual, imperishable
     person of heaven
     unperturbed
         by eleven inches of snow
         at Easter,
     undisturbed
         by bankruptcy,
         malignancy and
         moral complacency,
     undeterred
         by a forever dying body
         defaced by age from birth
         already
         and from then on and
         always?

Hasten the day of mystery!
Blow the trumpet soon
         to
         drop
         the
         chute
         of
         my
         cocoon

so I may fly to the comforting
  Person of Light
and greet all other things
bright and beautiful there.

Sometimes when two things happen on the same day, they don't sit right with each other.

I was reading the newspaper about a twenty million dollar contract agreed to by a major league baseball player and his club. Everyone was happy about the deal (good for but a few years), although the negotiations had been protracted and bitter. Now they could all put the hassle behind them and play ball.

My wife came home from work at 11:00 P.M. after a hard day of walking, charting, medicating, lifting, restraining, washing, quieting, assuring, and doing whatever else RN's do in geriatric nursing. As difficult as her task was, it at least didn't involve quite as much diaper changing and mess cleanup as was routinely done by the nurses' aids. What saints these aids were, my wife reported. She couldn't keep track of the numerous times she saw these dear humble saints go across the street to K-Mart on their lunch break to buy small presents for some patients whose families had forgotten them. With the sports pages still in my hand, I happened to ask my wife how much money these self-effacing, generous nurses' aids were paid. The answer I received set me to writing "Blasphemy," which I'm told has since appeared on the bulletin boards of more than one nursing home. The pay, incidentally, was minimum wage.

It saddens me some
to think that fans don't cheer
the nurse's aids
who dignify the lingering deaths
of medicates
urinating and vegetating
in joyless geriatric units.

It maddens me more
that crowds don't mass around
ignoble bedsides
to roar the praises
of minimum-wage nurses
enduring the smell and hell
of fleshless specimens
fighting off the end.

But give a youthful athlete
an agile body
and a ball in hand
    to hike
    and heave
        or dribble
        and dunk
            or hit
            and chase

                or kick
                and spike,
and millions will join
the senseless stampede
to screens and stadiums
where an afternoon's play
under silver domes
will secure multi-millions
of maximum pay,
and simultaneously engage
the fan's full praise.

God Almighty,
do you share my rage?

Four Poems Of Lament
For The Forgiveness Which Might Have Been

More often than I'd like to remember, I've been drawn as an arbitrator into the fray of a disintegrating marriage. Domestic war can be ugly and the weapons (verbal missives and swords) can be extremely lethal. But no weapon is so damaging as to put a marriage beyond the healing reach of mutual forgiveness. When pride is swallowed and hearts are renewed by the Spirit, then slingshots and swords can be set aside. Then deep wounds can be closed. On the numerous occasions of marital strife where I've seen God's Spirit prevail and bring healing, my spirit has been sent leaping. But there were those troubling times when the problems were not resolved. Then, sometimes, I needed the therapy of writing poetry, partially to steel the sinews of my own soul, but also to purge the confessions of my own sinfulness.

None of the following four poems, which had their genesis in some of the disappointments, were actually addressed and given to particular individuals or couples undergoing a divorce. All came to be written more in the nature of a personal lament, as I tried to identify with those wrestling with such evil forces as brought their marriages to an early sinking.

I cannot and may not judge the hearts of people who have experienced divorce. It is a deeply traumatizing experience

85

and is not always avoidable in this imperfect world. But I do feel sad for a few couples in my memory who, but for their prideful refusal to forgive, could almost certainly have started over. How close many others of us come to the brink of unforgiveness is a secret only we know. Jesus' warning to his disciples on the mount of temptation, "Watch With Me," is for everyone.

"Sweet And Sour"

Because I hate him,
I let him rob me
the nectareous delight of this luscious peach.
Sweet is sour
when I cannot forgive.

Because I hate him,
I let him ignite
the tinder of my vengeful feelings.
Sourness brought to him is all sweet to me
when the bitter is all his to experience.

Because I hate him,
I let him move my tongue
to caustic profanities.
Sweet thoughts convert quickly to sour words
when tossed about in a hostile mind.

86

Because I hate him,
I let him turn the cheerful harmony in my soul
into a dull cacophony of complaint.
Sour seems sweet and sweet turns to sour
when hatred is the blending agent.

Come, sweet Spirit,
take the sourness from my heart.
And set me free again
to love my enemy,
and to live without needing to hate him.

"Slingshot"

Some people win their wars so bluntly,
with bullets and bombs
and anti-missile-missile
sorts of things.

I do my fighting more discretely,
with a verbal slingshot
and a memory full of trivial tidbits.

Forgive me, Lord, the hurtful little missives
I've tossed out, like polished pebbles,
in casual conversation.

Disarm my tongue
and fill my mind
with bigger, better things.

"For Pride's Sake"

Sacrificed
my very soul
for Pride.
For her
    denied
my personal integrity,
    defied
my mate's offering
of forgiveness,
    decried
my children's believing love.

Large fees
to remand
to keep Pride
at hand
and command
her pretension
of trust.
Worth retention

88

is Pride?
But for
her attention
my heart's goodness
might not
have died.

"Watch With Me"

Watch with me then,
for tempter comes
with hemlock of happiness
in trade for cup of suffering.

Comes with hiss of force
and treacherous kiss,
with mix of strength and tenderness
to woo a counter-rebellion
of violence
to secure your rights.

Pick up the sword ever
and you only sever
the ear that hears.

Message of love
enforced by spears
mums God-fears,
gums the tears
welling to repentance.

Tempter can win
only if you beat him in.
But die for him
and your heat with sin
is over.

Watch with me then.
Be vigilant for those moments
when the yen to live
confronts your will to die.

Two Poems For My Colleagues
In Pastoral Care Ministry

Thank God one doesn't always have to have answers! What a relief it has been when I have discovered time and again, that what God has used to help someone was not my strength, not my aura of confidence, but my weakness and vulnerability.

Anyway, it's tiresome, indeed exhausting and exasperating, to always have to be the strong one. But because I have so often forgotten that, I have written for myself a poem of reminder, which I have also shared with several colleagues who have expressed to me that the poem soothed like fleece their guilt feelings for having needs of their own, and also gave them a sense of permission to let go.

"How Long Can I Be The Strong One?"

How long can I be the strong one?
They come to me, problem-plagued,
    depressed,
    grimly guilty,
    frantically fearful
        of divorce,
        of debt
        or damnation,

looking to me for . . . what?

    a pat answer,

    a prayer,

    a pat on the back,

    a word from God?

Often I have nothing more to give than

    tears and

    listening ears

which, even then, are bargains more than what

    they sought,

accomplishing more than pious answers could have

    ever taught.

When, dear God, may I weep for me

and ask them have their tears once join the flow

    of mine?

When may I be the weak and vulnerable and

    seeking one?

When will they understand that

my strength is measured

    in weakness?

When will I be humble and open enough

to let them test their strengths

on my not so infrequent failings?

Teach them the struggles of my soul to bear
and give me the grace to let them know my
    thorough humanness.

Another pitfall for people in my profession is to get buried in ecclesiastical busyness. Our time and energy is consumed by everything from committee meetings, to lecture preparations, to potluck suppers, to worship services, to who knows what else needs doing in the church. After a meeting of ministers gathered socially to view one of our colleague's slides of his holy land tour, I felt suddenly convicted by the selfishness and narrowness of my (and our) focus. My thoughts came to expression in the following not-so-soft poem:

"Holy Land"

At the church today
were slides of the holy land
and discussions of tombs
while people were dying
outside church rooms.

Messiah mostly missed
the churchy rooms
and chose to walk

uncommonly
on common roads
in common lives of ordinary people.

Now those common roads
and obscure histories of a little people
are holy
because he was there
outside the church's gates
to touch and transform them.

We've given tours,
shown slides,
written books,
voiced prophecies
about such things
for ages since.

God forgive us our religious remembrances
of holy things and holy days
and holy lands and holy tombs
which keep us so preoccupied
within the church's holy holy rooms
that our own common histories
and ordinary peoples and unholy lands
remain untouched by your sanctifying hands.

94

THREE POEMS FOR A FEW GOOD FRIENDS

The superficiality of all too many get-togethers with friends has often left me with a lingering hunger for something deeper. One evening my wife and I hosted a party for friends and decided to ask them to bring more than hors d'oeuvres. We invited them to bring something of themselves, something they had written or photographed or painted or quilted or memorized. We wanted to hear them sing their favorite song or play their favorite tape or tell their favorite story. We wanted friends to feel free to pray, to cry, to laugh together. It was an unforgettable evening. We were really friends that night! My contribution to the occasion was to dance the jitterbug with my wife and read a poem written especially for the initiation of the evening.

"Treasures Of The Deep"

Coy friends, but trust me a meagre bit,
open your shells a cautious slit,
show me white gifts so delicately pearled
in media of experience you've carefully curled
'round grains of irritation and yet of joy.
Ball of pied beauty's inside me too,
precious gem iridescent of gossamer hue
obscured to your view by my colorless case,

95

hidden for fear of its being too small,
uncultured or common, more base than all.

Let's plunge to the depths of our prismatic selves,
be wiser for lifting to lib'rating light
hurt-beauty we hide 'neath crustaceans of fright,
be richer for string of spun tears and pearled praise
we show now and wear to no friends' regrets.

One friend with whom I've had no trouble connecting
on a level of authentic humanness is dear old Cy Young. Cy
is a retired taxicab driver. He happens to be black. I love
the man. Whenever we have a rare opportunity to be
together, Cy becomes an open book of stories and dreams.
Cy's hero is Martin Luther King, and Cy has memorized
most of King's significant speeches. He has recited them
many times in parish churches where I have served, always
carrying a blessing to the worshippers.

"Big Black Cy"

Big Black Cy
tear in his eye
has dreams
Shares them with us whites
Makes you cry

to hear Big Black Cy
recite for memory
the poetry of Hughes
sermons of King
scriptures
of a vivid childhood

What is a man
white or black
without a dream

Big Black Cy
tear in his eye
has dreams
Love and peace
seem less like words
after Big Black Cy
has made his visit

If ever a man
can make me see
touch ought but white
it's got to be
Big Black Cy
tear in his eye
dreams in his soul

Friends, says C.S. Lewis, stand side by side to enjoy something in common. With Steve, my parish jogging partner, I ran side by side, literally. It was he who led me to attempt my one and only marathon. The most important benefit I derived from this incredibly painful experience was the good feeling of being supported by Steve's arms as I staggered across the finish line nearly four hours after the start. He, who had medaled, was proud that I had finished.

Another benefit of my insane effort was realized as well: a poem using the metaphor of the marathon to trace the race of faith through a year's segment of time.

"Marathon"

Short of breath
quickly
into oxygen debt
after long advent weekends
of mince meat and egg nog
we push our sluggish legs
along the snowy paths of January
First mile split
is slow
Slip on icy places a few times
when eyes are glazed
drugged by repetition
tired by obedience

Why go through this again
Do others ask this question

Got to run over the pain
run through it
spit on it
put it behind

Not so crowded on the course now
Spread out by differing limitations and assets
we nevertheless plod on
pulled along always by one or two
who keep our pace.
Good feeling not to be alone

Spring the roads are better
but potholes still a menace
Twist an ankle sure enough
when self-assured of way
Breezes at the back
slow the breathing
shorten the split

But then a u-turn at the road block
and good cadence is lost

A tragedy
A death
Unforeseen criticism
Loss of trust
No one along the course shouting encouragement
Slows us down
Maybe
puts us on our faces
cramped
unable to move

Heat, the summer's gift and curse
makes us feel light-footed
able to run forever
No worry for the road now
Our heads we have to worry about
Pressure builds with the pace
Slow down
run within yourself
rest for water
common sense says
Think we to listen
Not 'til waves of nausea
force Sabbath

Autumn splits are best
Trees are not so dark now
more colorful and welcoming
Life is a joy
Runner's high
sweeps us up hills
through the miles
Why isn't life always like this

Homestretch
through November and December winds
freezing rains
dark nights of the soul
tests the will to persevere

But what's that
A candle held by someone saying
"coming soon"
And then another telling us
to prepare for the end
By the time of the third
joy is returning
Hope follows with a rush
Crowds who came to cheer
the advent of our Forerunner
remain to praise us
to the finish

We have fought the good fight
finished the race
kept the faith
Now there is ready for us
a crown of righteousness
which the Lord the righteous judge
will award us on that Day
yes to all of us who loved his appearing
and ran our hearts out
to join him at the end
and share his glory

Two Poems For Kids Of The Parish

Some of my fondest memories of the last twenty-five years in the parish relate to shared experiences of frivolous fun with kids. Dancing wildly all over the place right in the middle of a youth choir rehearsal, playing hide-and-go-seek under the church pews after the rehearsal, and then pulling a prank on a good-natured janitor before we left for home were not activities kids expected to enjoy with the preacher. But happen they did.

For some reason or other kids often come to my mind when I'm on vacation. I'm not sure why. Maybe it's because everything lightens up a bit at vacation time. It was on one such vacation at Nettles Island in south Florida that I sat by the waterside, intermittently watching the fishermen feed the pelicans, and reading a collection of children's poems given to me by the church kids. It was Calvin Miller's delightful book, *When the Aardvark Parked On The Ark.* Inspired by the humorous/serious genre employed by Miller, and desirous of expressing appreciation to the kids for their gift to me, I wrote a poem for them:

"Pauly Pelican And Friends"

Pauly Pelican's favorite time
is when Freddy Fisherman comes at dusk

to clean sea trout at the water's edge.
Pauly's humongous mouth and endless neck
can inhale gigantic heads and tails
in one gargantuan gulp.
Trouble is, Pauly's friends appear in a sec'
to gobble the seafood entrees too,
especially when the servings are free, but few.

So when Freddy gets ready to lob out the bready,
all Pauly's friends become greedy and heady.
If one so happens to cob the trout,
but doesn't swallow it beyond a doubt,
in a flash will follow a graspy grouch
and rob the airmail from his hollow pouch.
But then this thief had better do
one mighty fast chug-a-lug-a-loo,
or other pesky pelicans will bug and clout him
and persistently try to mug and rout him,
almost like birds in a zoo.

Now astute ol' Pauly Pelican has played before
this fishy game along the shore.
When a choice trout snout descends
into Pauly's oral chute,
he extends far out his neck-bone flute,
flaps his wings to beat the hide,

104

wiggles his fanny feathers from side to side,
and in one great, gagging gulp
downs the trout in gastric pulp.

But Freddy, the friendly fisherman, and friends,
have a better way, they say.
They come together to baste and taste,
to brew and chew filets in stew,
never fretting conversational delays.

Like contented little birds,
Freddy Fisherman and friends chirp happily away,
while Pauly Pelican and friends salvage little more
than a distasteful burp today.

Better a modest meal shared
with friends,
than the whole head and tail snared
and swallowed alone.

During a subsequent vacation at my cottage on Lake Michigan, I had these kids on my mind again. So, as I watched rabbits scurrying about in the sand and bermuda beach grasses, and let myself think way back to my own childhood, I wrote for them another poem:

"Bold Billy Babbit And The Funny Bunny"

When bold Billy Babbit was barely a man,
his years all the span of thirteen,
he shot his very first bunny rabbit
right in the eyeballs between.
It seemed kinda funny almost
and even a reason to boast
to make a bunny do a silly flip
and take an instant, one-way trip
from its feet to its little bean.

The creature Billy left there
for a lean crow to clean,
and had never the slightest care
for what this death might mean.

Now that William Babbit's a little old man,
his year-span at eighty and three,
and barely able to see anymore,
except with the help of visine,
and his arm needing a sturdy crutch
on which occasionally to lean,
he has time enough, and even too much,
for his memories often to glean,
for second thoughts, so weighty and sore,
to silently intervene.

106

He sits apart and ponders now,
though it once did not at all seem,
if he had been just dastardly mean
when he had been but a half-grown lad,
not a tad past the age of thirteen,
and had thought it was so terribly funny
with his deadly twenty-two rifle gunny
to give a bunny a flippety-flip
from its feet to its little bean.

PART FOUR: FAMILY

Paradoxically, though life in the family seems often to be the most humdrum affair, it is also the domain where the decibels of joy and laughter reach to their ecstatic limit, and where the lower registers of pain and grief become sighs too deep for even the most sensitive ears.

Suddenly, in the midst of life's boring, everyday sameness comes the delightful tale of a son's vision at naptime, the ecstasy of a moment of emotional intimacy with one's mate, the unexpected diagnosis of a young nephew's cancer or the abrupt telephone call of a father's death. These and other surprises turn the ordinary home into a light realm of wonder and celebration, and then in a moment, into a dark den of sorrow.

Such intensities as these are the stuff of which poetry is made, or should I say, the intensities to which poetry can best speak in its own "sinews of fleece" kind of way.

Jesus Is Tickling Me

The height of my son today at six foot four reminds me that it was really quite a few years ago when we shared a moment of imagination and good humor at his naptime.

The experience of that moment, however, is as poignant in my memory as if it happened but a second ago. It keeps reminding me that the innocent, expectant faith of children gives them more receptive eyes and ears than we adults whose spiritual sensitivities are jaded by our practical realism and acquired skepticism. It reminds me too that Jesus linked entrance into the kingdom of heaven with becoming as a little child.

Literally thousands of people through the years have listened with amusement (quiet mirth) and with musement (profound reflection) to the reading of the poem "Jesus Is Tickling Me" which became part of my prayer diary on that unforgettable day when the Friend of Children paid a visit.

Strange thing happened this noon.
Still has me smiling . . . And wondering a bit.

My son wouldn't settle down for his nap.
Giggling and chuckling infectiously
and shaking his bed with laughter,
he aroused my curiosity sufficiently

to lure me to the vicinity of his bedroom.
I pushed my poker face through his door
and said as sternly as I could manage:
"What are you giggling about?"

"Jesus is tickling me,"
he replied with an innocent grin and cheeks
flushed from a recent tussle.

What could I say, Jesus?
Were you tickling him?
My rational brain said, "Not possible!"
My heart said, "Well, maybe. . . ."

I know you have a special way with children,
and children with you.
I know the door of a child's faith
would not be closed to an afternoon visitation by you.

But at the time
I didn't know quite how to respond.
Searching for words,
and with one hand raised over my smiling face,
I said finally, "Son,
you and Jesus both settle down for a while."

110

Jesus, I hope you didn't mind.
I thought my boy needed a little rest.

I wonder, though,
maybe I should have paused to question him
like the elders did of you in the temple
when you were still a boy
filled with fresh revelations from God.

INNOCENCE

Looking backward a couple decades to my married daughter's childhood brings to mind the picture of "Innocence" I saw and wrote about when she fell asleep in her highchair at the dinner table.

What a blessing to be able to nod off and not worry about what you might lose control of!

Innocence is like a child
asleep in dinner chair
with glass of milk in outstretched hand, while
loss of same is like a man, awake,
staggering through life down ulcerous path,
unable for slightest moment to break his step
lest crystal cup of life's investments
fall-slip from clutching hand
and shatter then in lustful dream of better things.

WAITING

One Christmastide evening in recent memory my family had a fight. No big deal. Every family has its spats. One occasion of disharmony shouldn't be over-magnified in its significance—especially if it took place in the letdown period after the high of Christmas had passed.

True. Unkind words and insensitive acts at a time when everyone was dragged out by the holidays and tired of all the togetherness are certainly somewhat excusable and can be readily forgiven. And such blowups are a universal experience with families.

But not true. If spats come to be expected as normal, then something abnormal becomes normal. A family can slip then into the pathology of accepting all the fighting and bickering as the way all families are. The tragedy in such thinking is that precious moments ripe with potential for love and celebration become wasted. Before anyone wakes up to realize what has been squandered and lost, the family has long since been dispersed by college and marriage and death.

So every squabble is serious. Tomorrow is never soon enough for love.

So soon the decades advance,
and we're found lying perchance

in pain, waiting death's merciful lance,
while ghosts of a poignant past
haunt us with melancholy.

We'll remember one Christmastide
when we were so quick to chide,
so careless of those fragile moments
together, at a warm hearth beside,
as winter's fury was spent outside.

We'll wish to live that best time over,
love those near as we could but wouldn't.
Now is the day to say our love:
we shouldn't wait. . . .
We shouldn't wait.

Back in the years when my wife, Faith, and I were still courting in my little blue VW bug, I used to catch her staring at me. I'd feel her gaze studying me, and suddenly I'd look over toward her. Her face would leap into a smile of affection. What a joy, what a mystery to be thus admired and even adored, I thought. How could this be happening to me?

"Because Your Face"

I loved you then because your face . . .
it leaped at me
and splashed me with the feeling fresh
that I was all the sailing raft
you ever in your highest waves
had wished the Wind would breeze you;
and I felt joy to know
that I was thus a vessel in a deeper love
than hitherto had held me up
in all the shallow waters
where punctured hopes lay buried.

Now, these many years later, after we've come to know each other so intimately, I find *myself* doing a fair bit of

115

staring, fascinated by the depth, lured by the mystery of this familiar lover.

"Of Love And Mystery"

I want
and do not want
to know
the burning core
and polar reach
    of you.

Exploring carefully
the labyrinthine trails
of your verdant, complex self,
I, better than any other,
could be a blindfolded guide
for numerous, backpacking biographers
doing their detailed histories
    of you.

Yet, deep
is the forest of being,
and your mysteries beyond
woo like a magic wand;
they keep my feet from tiring

of the more familiar paths
I need to walk
before aspiring
to stalk
another unseen part
  of you.

Knowing so much
of what little I know
of the infinite more
there is still to know,
I, suspended in love
between history and mystery,
am drawn but fearfully
to continue the search.

Marriage is the blending of two radically different per-
sonalities into a single life plan. The blending, over a long
period of years, can be so thorough that it may even seem at
times difficult to identify where the borders of individuali-
ty are. Yet, at other times the utter difference of the other
person becomes so obvious that the borders may even begin
to feel like Berlin walls. Through all the fits and starts of
closeness and distance, the discovery is made that only
mutual submission to Christ can draw and keep a husband
and wife together.

"Triangle"

From
the lines
of right angle
to husband and wife
God draws the hypotenuse
of opposites desiring oneness
reducing the span of distance from
his Son to a common point of submission

Being together *is* the joy, as Solomon wrote about in his *Song Of Songs*. A quiet evening of reading that song, while my wife sat nearby knitting, moved me to write:

"Because The Joy Is You"

A stroll on the beach alone
is a stroll on the beach alone.

But when with you, my love,
I feel within the stirring of bazaar fancies.
Chasing the sandpiper and
falling spastically in the water
are not things I think to enjoy alone.

Because the joy is you.

Even Solomon could pursue the unkingly sport
of catching vineyard foxes
and refreshing his maiden with apples and raisins
when love brought him afflatus of spirit.

Your love opens my eyes
and lets me see the beauty
in everything.

A walk with you in the city
on a cluttered avenue
is an experience of discovering delicate flowers
hidden among the broken beer bottles.
Alone, I see only the smog
and feel oppressed by tall buildings.

A night at home together
is to discover, like Solomon's maiden,
that "our couch is green;
     the beams of our house are cedar,
     our rafters are pine."

A night alone,
and the colors of green and delightful wood smells
seem strangely elusive.

Because the joy is you.

GIVING BIRTH TO SELF

Ethicists distinguish between need love and gift love.

One of life's richest paradoxes is that need love's thirst is best assuaged when the need lover answers the thirst of another need lover with the gift of an outpoured self.

This paradox, and its delicate interplay of proliferating needs arising out of the act of love, was running through my mind one Mother's Day as I wrote "Giving Birth To Self" for my mother.

From needful sower-husband
love found its way to you
a seed sent your ovum soil
multiplied beyond a thousandfold
to miracle of me
praising now your motherhood

You needed baby me
to be a woman feeling difference
had to give me birth
for giving birth to you
yourself

Self's then most fulfilled
when yielded

opened for the harvest
fruit
of children
like the likes of me
needing you
mother
needing you
lover
needing you
other

So
are we born
and reborn
of need
the seed

Three Poems In My Father's Memory

What I remember best about my father is that he always looked, spoke and thought up to me, though for a good many years he was taller than I. I have long since regarded my father's example as my inheritance of honor, for what is honor but the attitudinal posture of looking up.

Wherein lies a beautiful truth: kids who treat their parents well are the very same as have themselves been made to feel special by their parents. Respect is contagious.

"Face I See Again"
My father was of men
most sovereign
because he stood to them
the farthing
when they and he subconsciously
thought up or down in speaking.

My father,
he looked up to men,
and his face—
minted in my memory—
I see again in treasury
in the faces of my children.

The face I see,
naivity,
can be amused—
gemmate to joy—
with a penny's worth
of verbal toy.

The face I see,
credulity,
accepts a person
because he's there
and thereby worthy
of listening fare.

The face I see,
expectancy,
presumes in man
such gold supply
as a smile's worth
of trust can buy.

Honor was only one part of the inheritance I received from my father. For I the pastor have learned more about visiting the sick from my dad, a humble meatcutter, than I have from any shepherding class or seminar on practical theology. My dad, who passed away in 1966 at age fifty-four,

123

was a quiet man not given to wordiness. A high school graduate only, he looked up to me with pride as the son who "had gone on to school." To be sure, in worldly terms I went much farther than my father; yet, it was he more than any who, in his Christlike humanness, taught me a most vital lesson about ministering to hurting people.

It all happened this way. In 1961 Dad had his first heart attack. He survived to experience the love and concern of many townspeople who came to visit him in the hospital. This outpouring of love so impressed him that he felt called to become a visitor of the sick. No, he wasn't a church Elder, and he hadn't ever done much of this visiting before in his life. But Christ said: "Care!" and Dad cared. He visited everybody. It made no difference whether they were neighbors or strangers. For six years, before a second heart attack took his life, Dad made regular visits to the hospital located in a city seventeen miles away.

The *fact* that he visited was already model enough for me. But there was still another lesson in the *style* of the visits. Dad usually wouldn't say much. He felt awkward and ill-equipped to say the right words. He would shuffle his feet as he stood at a sufferer's bedside. There would be tears in his eyes. He understood pain, and the sick person knew it. Occasionally, Dad would offer a prayer or read a psalm, but most often he simply left behind the overwhelming impression that someone cared. His tears were gift enough.

For me, the pastor, it is not a problem to breeze into a hospital room and deposit God's word of mercy on a suffering soul. But Dad taught me that, in doing this, I have not done all. For it isn't enough to enter the room; I must enter the bed and, indeed, the skin of the patient. Doctors enter the body. It is for me to make entry into the very soul. My empathy is a sharper scalpel than my pastoral rap.

Dad's example to me is summarized in a poem I wrote in his memory many years after his death.

"The Visit"

I hear you.
You are saying, "Don't speak;
just listen to my pain and
tend awhile to my bitterness.

Just shuffle your feet and feel
speechless before me
in the awesome company
of my struggle."

I hear you.
You are saying, "No need to smile;
just let my tears
condense a drop from your eyes.

Just wring your hands and feel, yes,
awkward before me
for lack of words
to make me right easily."

I hear you.
You are saying, "Be still;
comfort me with presence
and heal me with silence.

Your touch is strength enough
just now.
Later you can talk your answers
and I will listen."

It was a wretched day when my dad died. Waves of grief
swept over me, pounding me senseless for three days and
nights. But Dad's funeral and burial was like the renewal of
Easter for me. With the corpse, the coffin and all the other
stark reminders of death's finality present, I could think of
nothing but Dad's resurrection. With the body of this
upward-looking man now lying prone before everyone, I
smiled to think that he was still passing on the lesson of
honor. Of course, deep inside I knew that the last rights,
the rights Dad never had insisted on in his relationships
with others, were now truly his.

126

"Last Rights"

Old in bed chamber he lies, his
skin grey-iced as he dies;
wise that life's sin he conceived, he
told to the Christ he believed.

Cold in steel coffin he lies, his
ears now numb to good-byes;
like-wise to tears of bereaved, to
gold of the dumb, death-deceived.

Holed in dirt graveyard he lies, his
life excised of all ties;
like-wise of strife he received, but
bold now to rise, fall-relieved.

Jerry's life was full: a loving wife to partner with him in ministry; four children delayed in coming, but so very much alive in spite of once-imagined barrenness; a mother who modeled grace and charity; a career in ministry flourishing with published books and teacher-of-the-year awards; fond appreciations from beneficiaries of his teaching and counsel.

But then there was Friday, the dark night when mother, wife and four-year-old daughter were suddenly terminated by a speeding and intoxicated driver.

Such loss is unimaginable to me. And its consequent grief I could only observe as a helpless comforter who flew to Washington State to be with Jerry in his pain.

Two scenes, portraits of grief, stand out in my memory of those awful few days. The first was at the mortuary on the morning of the funeral. After much inner debate, Jerry had decided he needed the last visit, the last touch, the last sight of his dear ones. He asked me to be present and stand with him there as he met his grief face to face, and began to find closure.

"Closure"

Did hands, folded, slightly move just now?
Did eyelashes flicker, but barely?

128

No. Lifeless caricatures,
they lie like stuffed dolls.

Everything's so real, so very unreal
without the breath:
manikins cosmetologized,
propped with hidden wires.
Yet, what urgent messages,
what wailings heavy with pain,
what tear-gales impelled by grief,
must these mummies receive.

Not a flinch of response, though;
just a listening and caring imagined
from the memories of a thousand smiles
and soothing looks.

Still, there's comfort somehow
in visiting once more these temples,
and directing through the veils beyond
laments of love.

Our journey east heads straight to west
as Friday touches Easter.
And tombs are closed, enforcing night,
before they're opened to the light.

The second scene occurred a few hours later at the graveyard where I led the services of committal. By this time, it seemed, Jerry's heart was nearly cried out. He pulled me aside just before we left the caskets behind to tell me he was falling down into a dark pit—maybe of Sheol. I sensed then the depth of the grief I had been observing in him and which he would carry from that place for the rest of his life.

"Grief To Carry"

Heart cried out:
dehydrated of tears,
left with the brine
and nausea
coming in waves
of barren wretching
and speechless wailing.

Absolute loneliness,
torturous solitude,
endless reaching out to hold
the arms of comforters
just not enough,
just not the same.

Emotions cold as north,
then hot as south,
arid, then drenching,
tactile, then numb,
turbulent and eruptive,
transparent and unmasked.

Contraction of soul
engaging every nerve and muscle;
centripetal suction of spirit
pulling the flesh around itself
in the instinct to protect;
exhaustion in the marrow.

Such is the sorrow he has carried,
the grief he has borne.
By the grace, then, of such understanding,
new savor of hope arises
from the grief assimilated
though never forgotten.

A man of deep faith is this cousin of mine. Our last
long-distance phone conversation led me to sense that the
savor of hope was emerging from the brine. God be blessed!

Two Poems In Memory Of A Little Saint

At first it seemed that Adam's cancer wasn't too serious. The removal of a kidney was major surgery, but the prognosis was good. And Adam had all the vitality of a six year old. Still, the dragon wouldn't lie down. Cut off his head, and weeks later he would appear headless, but alive, and with a firm grip on some new part of Adam's body. Tumor here. Tumor there. It was like the dragon had a tail of fire which set off a rage of cancer cells wherever it mindlessly struck.

This duel with death went on and on, putting Adam in numerous hospitals, subjecting him to repeated surgeries and, of course, to the poisonous, potential cure meant to kill the dragon yet so invasive to a little boy's own appearance and sense of dignity.

Adam's dad and mom prayed, struggled, cried from wondering: Where have cancer's fingers reached? And how tenacious will be their hold? Is this the kind of leech that hangs on defying every scalpel, every poison? How severe will be the pain? How painful the attempted cure? Our beloved son, can we let him go? And he us? What is God's part in all this? Whenever the fears would focus on Adam, whether expressed by parents, family or hospital staff, Adam would always lead everyone through the fog of fear and doubt. He trusted Jesus implicitly, and he explicitly challenged everyone else to do the same. Two nurses at a University hospital were led to Christ by Adam's believing and bold witness.

Adam died at seven years of age, during the week of Yom Kippur, the Jewish festival of the atonement.

God gave me two poems for my little nephew, the first written a few months before his death, the second, written and read as a prayer at the memorial service held in Adam's honor.

"Adam"

Little boy
but seven,
on a scale of one to ninety
thereabouts,
cancer can't have you,
nor yet can heaven.

Not if one and one makes two
and blue is blue,
a peaceful hue,
and things make sense
and kids grow up
as they're supposed to do.

Only old fools lie down
weak, balded,
stooped by pain,
thinned, thinking always of dying.

Life is for the beginning,
death for the ending.

How so wise
so calm
little boy?
How so bold to push your shoulders back
and go for it one more time,
braving the poison potential cure?
Months and months more
of cycling caps in bed
and tasteless treats,
playing hide-and-go-seek with
cousins' colds,
learning and living
mostly with mommy,
mostly alone.

Little boys
can't be veterans
of cancer wars.

Little boys
can't soften nurses' hearts
to Jesus.

Little boys
can't say it's okay
and not to worry
to big daddys
sobbing
and big doctors
weeping in the hallway.

Are you a little boy, Adam?
You seem as old as your name,
almost ageless in a way.
Little boy
so old
so young,
you've given so much life.
Can't you have a little back?

"From Seven Years To Eternity"

Cancer-tested,
on the seventh year
he rested, Lord,

entered his vested sabbath
like the slaves set free,
the debtors forgiven.

We hoped for Jubilee,
for years seven times seven
at least,
but you insisted
on early redemption.

Persistent God you've proved to be,
seeking the lap-side company
of this little saint.

God, we wanted him too,
fought to save him,
prayed desperately for life,
cried, yes, sometimes angrily, for mercy,
tried every medical, spiritual remedy.

Ola k̵ala. All is well.
You've won.
But so it seems has this first-born son,
stretching his meagre seven years
by witness born of bold spiritual naivete
into everlasting significance

136

for who knows how many nurses
and doctors and aunts and uncles
and dads and moms and other kids.

Seven years was enough eternity
for this little guy,
enough to do more for us and you
than his namesake could have done
did he still survive his start at Eden.

Thank you, God,
for Adam Knol
who touched the soul
of us.

Now hold him to yourself . . . there,
and us to Adam's faith . . . here,
till at reunion . . . then,
in that death-free sabbath land
we see and understand.